LEARN

INDONESIAN

FOR LOWER BEGINNER LEVEL 1

SPEAK INDONESIAN PHRASE BOOK

MOHD MURSALIN SA'AD

Copyright

Title: Learn Indonesian for Lower Beginner level 1

Subtitle: Speak Indonesian Phrase Book

Series: Indonesian for Lower Beginner

Publisher: LETS Learn Effective Training Skills
Reg No: 53309248E
Written by the Author
Mohd Mursalin Sa'ad
Website: LETS-360.COM

National Library Board, Singapore Cataloguing in Publication Data

Name(s): Mohd Mursalin Sa'ad.
Title: Learn Indonesian for lower beginner. Level 1 : speak Indonesian phrase book / Mohd Mursalin Sa'ad.
Other Title(s): Indonesian for lower beginner
Description: Singapore : LETS Learn Effective Training Skills, [2026] | In English and Indonesian.
Identifier(s): ISBN 978-981-94-3227-1 (paperback) | 978-981-94-3228-8 (ebook)
Subject(s): LCSH: Indonesian language--Textbooks for foreign speakers--English. | Indonesian language--Conversation and phrase books--English.
Classification: DDC 499.22182421--dc23

LEARN INDONESIAN for LOWER BEGINNER LEVEL 1

It is time to Speak Indonesian
and reinvent your life

LETS

Preface

The author of this book has gone through the learning process of learning a foreign language, thus, through the years of experience he formulated this small handbook for your new language discoveries. He understands that learning a foreign language is not an easy task, but with perseverance and discipline, he reckons any person can really learn and speak a foreign language.

The book is a series of language learning lessons. Each lesson consists of the following: explanation of the lesson, transcript of dialogues, Indonesian translation in English, key phrase, simple sentences, and detailed explanation of important grammar concepts. The author highlights simple phrases at the beginning of every lesson, for students to memorize prior reading the dialogues. It is critical that students memorize new words that have functions like using the phrase in speaking. Words which have no meaning may be rejected by the brain and difficult to recall. Thus, the author recommends that the student understands the words, memorizes it and use the phrase in daily speaking.

The dialogues will be more beneficial for the new foreign language learner with consistent practice, being creative in your learning approach is a key to success, we recommend that you record your own voice on the mobile phone or any recording device for you to listen to and getting your ears accustomed to the Indonesian language accent. Not to mention answering some questions from students with simple clarification.

You will learn Indonesian expression, current events, and capable to express question and replies when speaking with Indonesian people on the streets. and more. The system will get you speaking Indonesian in your first lesson. Help you memorize simple phrase, recall words and most importantly speaking with fluent

Indonesian even though you have not mastered the Indonesian alphabets reading and writing.

Disclaimer: This book is not intended to teach you Indonesian alphabets and writing system. If you want to learn Indonesian writing system, then this book is not for you.

The author suggests that the potential learner who will succeed in learning the new foreign language depends entirely on his discipline and commitment to learn.

Here are some facts to achieve your potential:

- □ You need to allocate time to revise new lessons.
- □ A phone to save audio and listen when you travel.
- □ A small pocket notebook to write down new words.
- □ Practice writing and spelling Indonesian words.
- □ Aspiration to learn Indonesian.
- □ Books as reference

- ☐ Engaged with the Indonesian language by Speaking Indonesian daily and reading more reference books.
- ☐ Believed that you can achieve the foreign language feat, because others in foreign continents and across the globe in Asia speak Indonesian.

Send our book links If you find this book beneficial to you and may help other foreign language learners to enhance their language skills.

From the desk of the Author

Mohd Mursalin Sa'ad

Damascus, Syria.

How to use this Book?

This book is written in series and has 15 topics, every topic is designed with simple phrases to help you memorize and understand better. You need to master the first lesson, with that said able to use the phrase, and from that onwards more phrases will be introduced to You in stages.

This book, "Learn Indonesian for Lower Beginner level 1" is for total beginner to help students launch their Indonesian speaking skills without boundaries or has prior knowledge of the Indonesian letters and writing system. Don't start your Indonesian lessons by learning letters and writing system, because learning letters will hinder your studies. Keep learning the speaking lessons, and do not be discouraged if you have not mastered some of the lessons, because our mind takes time to absorb and master it. Words that have meanings and are used daily will have better potential to recall.

Create a journal for you to write words in Indonesian. Observe the Indonesian words and try to recall the phrase in English.

We also added some questions and tips for you to understand the expressions and usage of the Indonesian grammar rules.

At the end of every topic, we insert a list of phrases for you to recall the essential phrase. If your e-book has audio capability, you may hear the phrase in Indonesian, listen and understand the phrase. Repeat it again to ensure that you know every phrase. If you don't understand some phrases, no worries, repeat reading the topic on more time.

Cheers to your success!

Author: Mohd Mursalin Sa'ad

Table of Content

Lesson 1: Common Greetings

Indonesian greetings are an essential part of daily communication and social etiquette. Here are the most common greetings based on the time of day:

Essential Phrase

	Indonesian	**English**
1	Halo	*"Hello "*
2	Selamat pagi	*"Good morning."*
3	Selamat siang	*"Good afternoon"*
4	Selamat sore	*"Good evening"*
5	Selamat malam	*"Good night"*
6	sampai berjumpa lagi	*"See you soon"*
7	Selamat tinggal	*"Goodbye"*

Dialogue Between Sara, Bob and Ella

Setting: At the campus. *In this dialogue, Sara says hello to Bob.*

Sara: (Halo.) – *"Hello."*

Bob: (Selamat pagi.) – *"Good morning."*

In the evening after school

Sara: (sampai berjumpa lagi.) – *"See you soon."*

Bob: (Selamat tinggal.) – *"Goodbye."*

Bob: (Selamat sore.) – *"Good evening."*

Sara: (Halo, Bob! Apa kabar) – *"Hello, Bob! How are you?"*

Bob: (Saya baik-baik saja, terima kasih. Dan Anda?) – *"I'm good, thank you. And you?"*

Sara: Saya juga baik-baik saja, terima kasih. – *"I'm also good, thank you."*

Bob: (Bagaimana harimu?) – *"How's your day?"*

Sara: (Hariku menyenangkan, terima kasih. Dan bagaimana denganmu?) – *"My day is good, thank you. And yours?"*

Bob: (Hari saya juga menyenangkan, terima kasih sudah bertanya.) – *"My day is also good, thank you for asking."*

Sara: (Baiklah, aku harus pergi sekarang. Selamat tinggal, Bob.) – *"Well, I have to go now. Goodbye, Bob."*

Bob: 9Selamat tinggal, Sara! Terima kasih atas percakapannya!) – *"Goodbye, Sara! Thank you for the conversation!'*

Sara: (Sama-sama! Sampai jumpa lagi – *"You're welcome! See you later."*

Bob: (Sampai jumpa lagi.) – *"See you later."*

Recall: The Indonesian phrase and understand the English translation

1 Halo。

Hello

2 Selamat pagi
Good morning.

3 Selamat sore
Good evening.

4 Selamat malam
Good night

Lesson 2: Expressing Gratitude

The expression below is appropriate on many occasions.

Essential Phrase:

	Indonesian	**English**
1	Ini dia	*"Here is "*
2	Kopi anda	*"Your coffee."*
3	Teh anda	*"Your Tea."*
4	Terima kasih	*"Thank you"*
5	Terima kasih kembali	*"You're welcome"*
6	Gula	*"Sugar"*
7	Krimer	*"Creamer"*
8	Bagaimana saya bisa membantu Anda?"	*"How can I help you?"*
9	secangkir kopi	*"a coffee"*
10	omelet	*"an omelette"*

11	Saya ingin kopi dan omelet.	*"I would like a coffee and an omelette"*
12	Tolong	*"please"*
13	Sebentar	*"a moment"*

Take note:

You get a hot cup of coffee at the café (*kafe/ warung*)

Dialogue Between barista and customer saying, "thank you".

Setting: At a local café. In this dialogue, Sara expresses her gratitude to the barista for serving her coffee.

Barista: {Selamat pagi! Ada yang bisa saya bantu?) – *"Good morning! How can I help you?"*

Lucas: (Selamat pagi. Saya ingin memesan kopi dan omelet). – "*Good morning. I would like a coffee and an omelet, please.*"

Barista: (Mohon tunggu sebentar.) – *"Just a moment, please."*

Barista: (Ini kopimu) – "*Here is Your coffee*"

Sara: (Terima kasih) – *"Thank You"*

Barista: (Terima kasih kembali). – *"You're welcome."*

(Ini gula) – *"This is sugar"*

(Ini krimer) – *"This is creamer"*

Is it necessary to clasp both hands when greeting Indonesian people on the streets?

While it's not strictly necessary to clasp both hands when greeting Indonesian people on the streets. This is a common and respectful gesture in Indonesia culture. However, waving your hands to say hello, is accepted.

In everyday encounters with strangers or acquaintances on the street, a simple nod of the head or smile is often sufficient as a sign of politeness and acknowledgment.

Never use sign language gesture or pointing your fingers at others, it is a sign of argument or confrontation. Remember to be respectful and considerate in your interactions.

Generally, Indonesians are nice and courteous people.

Practice this phrase (I want) "Saya ingin"

place a noun after the phrase "ingin"

Kopi (coffee), *omelet* (*omelette*), *teh* (tea), *susu* (milk)

Recall: The Indonesian phrase and understand the English translation

1. Ini kopi mu

   Here is your coffee

2. Terima kasih

   Thank you

3. Terima kasih kembali

   You're welcome

4. Ini gula

   This is sugar

5. Ini krimer

   This is creamer

Lesson 3: Apologizing

Here is a simple phrase to use if you want to say, "Excuse me" or "sorry."

1. (Permisi).- "Excuse me"
2. (Maaf) – "Sorry"

How do you use (Permisi)

If you intent to leave you seek permission by saying (Permisi) – Excuse me.

The difference between (permisi) and (maaf)

(Permisi Pak) – Excuse me Sir.

Whereas the phrase (Maaf) means that you are sorry

(Maaf, saya terlambat) – "I'm sorry, I'm late."

Getting Someone's Attention: "Permisi" can be used to politely get someone's attention or to ask for assistance:

(Permisi, saya ingin meminta bantuan.") – *"Excuse me, I have a favour to ask."*

(Permisi, bolehkah saya duduk di sini?) – *"Excuse me, may I sit here."*

Simple Phrase

	Indonesian	**English**
1	Saya minta maaf	*"I'm sorry_"*
2	Aku terlambat	*"I'm late."*
3	Saya ingin meminta bantuan.	*"I have a favour to ask"*
4	Tidak, tidak apa-apa.	*"No, it's okay"*

5	Aku benar-benar minta maaf	*"I'm really sorry"*
6	Bolehkah saya duduk disini?	*"May I sit here?"*
7	sama sekali tidak mengapa	*"Absolutely no problem"*
8	Tolong	*"Please"*
9	Duduklah bersamaku	*"Sit with me."*
10	Terima kasih banyak	*"Thank you very much"*
11	Tidak masalah	*"No worries"*

Dialogue Between Ella and passenger saying, "sorry".

Setting: *On a crowded train. In this scenario, Ella apologizes for bumping into a passenger on a crowded train. The passenger reassures Ella that it's not a big deal, to which Ella expresses her gratitude for the understanding.*

Ella: Accidentally bumps into someone while entering the train

(Saya minta maaf) – *"I'm sorry"*

Passenger: (Tidak, apa-apa). – *"No, it's okay."*

Ella: (Aku benar-benar minta maaf). – *"I'm really sorry."*

Take note: you may add with these phrases with (Pak) "Sir" or (Bu) "Madame"

Setting: On a crowded restaurant. In this scenario, Bob apologizes for requesting a table on a crowded restaurant. Ella reassures Bob that it's not a big deal, to which Bob expresses his gratitude for the understanding.

Bob: (Permisi, bolehkah saya duduk di sini?) – *"Excuse me, may I sit here."*

Ella: (Sama sekali tidak mengapa) – *"Absolutely no problem"*

(Duduklah bersamaku) – *"Please, sit with me."*

Bob: (Terima kasih banyak.) – *"Thank you very much."*

Ella: (Tidak masalah) – *"No worries"*

Take note: The locals usually say the phrase "tidak" with "***ngak***" such as:

Ngak masalah Pak – *"No worries, Sir"*

Ngak bisa – *"Cannot"*

Ngak bisa pak/bu – "Cannot sir/madame"

Recall: The Indonesian phrase and understand the English translation

1 Maaf, permisi.

Sorry, Excuse Me.

2 tidak apa-apa
it's okay

3 Aku benar-benar minta maaf
I'm really sorry

4 Maaf, Saya terlambat
I'm sorry, I'm late.

5 Permisi, saya ingin meminta bantuan.
Excuse me, I have a favour to ask.

6 Terima kasih
Thank you

Lesson 4: Introduce someone.

In this lesson, you will learn phrase to introduce someone in Indonesian. And using possessive pronouns?

Essential Phrase:

	Indonesian	**English**
1	Ini	*"This is"*
2	Buku Bob	*"Bob's book"*
3	Teman Mary	*"Mary's friend"*
4	Mobil Tom	*"Tom's car"*
5	Abang saya	*"My brother"*

In Indonesian language, you can introduce someone by first saying the noun and then saying their name Here are some examples.

1. This is Bob's book.
   - (Ini adalah **buku** Bob..)
2. She is Mary's friend.
   - (Dia adalah **teman** Mary.)
3. That is Tom's car.
   - (Itu **mobil** Tom..)

4. He is **my** brother.
    - (Dia adalah saudara laki-laki saya.)

In these examples, possessive pronouns (e.g., "Bob's," "Mary's," "Tom's," "my") are formed by combining the person's name with a noun to indicate ownership or association. With that said, to say a possessive form in Indonesian is really easy, First, you need to know the noun such as, (book, friend, car, brother) then the second word is to place the person’s name.

Here is a simple example

1	*Kemeja* John	*John's shirt*
2	*Sepeda* Thomas	*Thomas' motorbike*
3	*Kacamata* Sheila	*Sheila's glasses*
4	*Ponsel* John	*John's mobile phone*
5	*Kamera* Daniel	*Daniel's camera*

Pronouns is easy such as:

(Dia) refers to He/she

(Saya/Aku) refers to My/me

Whereas demonstrative nouns consists of near and far

1	(ini)	This (near)
2	(itu)	That (far)

So, how do you implement this demonstrative nouns?

1	(Ini buku Saya)	-This is my book
2	(Ini tas Saya)	-This is my bag
3	(Ini mobil Saya)	-This is my car

Isn't that simple, now how about some variations of pronouns; We are going to insert the (nya) to point to a possessive pronoun for male and female. So, that means the (nya) refers to he/she.

(1)

Itu ponsel Fatima-*That is fatima's mobile phone*

Itu ponsel**nya**– *That is her mobile phone*

(2)

Ini kacamata – *These glasses*

Itu kacamata Sheila – *Those are Sheila's glasses*

Itu kacamata**nya**.– *That is her glasses*

Take note, that to transform “fatima’s mobile phone” into “her mobile phone” you need to insert the possessive pronouns, (**nya**) at the end of an object to refer it to (her)

The same concept applies if it is (his) such as:

(1) Buku**nya**–his book
(2) Mobil**nya** – His car
(3) Ponsel**nya** – Her mobile phone
(4) Rumah**nya** – Her house

Another type of demonstrative nouns is “here and there”

Let us observe the structure of the sentences. We use (Sini) to refer to “here” and we say, (Situ) to refer to “there”. (Sana) to refer to something further away, we use “over there”.

1) Buku di sini – *Here is the book*
2) Ponsel di sini – *Here is the mobile phone*
3) Toko di situ – *The shop is there*

4) Kafe di situ – *The café is there*
5) Mobil di sana (further) – *The car is over there*
6) Rumah di sana (further) – *The house is over there*

Recall: The Indonesian phrase and understand the English translation

1 Ini adalah buku Bob。
This is Bob's book

2 Dia adalah teman Mary
She is Mary's friend

3 Itu mobil Tom。
That is Tom's car.

4 Dia adalah saudara laki-laki saya
He is my brother

Lesson 5: What's your name?

Here's a basic phrase for introducing yourself and asking for someone's name in Indonesian:

Here is a simple phrase to use if you want to say, "What's your name?"

1. (Siapa nama**mu**?).- "What's your name?"
2. (Siapa nama **dia**?) – "What's his/her name?"

Essential Phrase:

Indonesian	**English**
Saya	*"I am"*
[Nama anda]	*[Your Name].*
Dan kamu?	*"And you?"*
Saya John	*"I am John."*

How to insert your name?

1. (Nama Saya [Your Name]) – "I am [Your Name]."
2. (Dan kamu?) – "And you?"
3. What's your name?) – "What's your name?"

So, for example, if your name is John, you can say:

- (Saya John.) – "I am John."
- (Dan kamu?) – "And you?"

This is a simple way to introduce yourself and politely ask for the other person's name.

Take note:

If you intend to say "*your name*" you insert the pronouns (mu) at the end of the word (nama). So, it becomes like this, (nama**mu**) – "*your name*"

And if you intend to refer to male or female you insert at the end of the word (nama) + (**dia**). So, it becomes (nama **dia**) and refers to "his name" if it is male person, and to refer to "her name" using the same concept (nama **dia**).

Simple Phrase:

	Indonesian	English
1	Saya Bob	*"I'm Bob"*
2	Senang temu anda	*"Nice to meet you."*
3	Halo, Bob	*"Hello, Bob."*
4	Terima kasih kembali	*"You're welcome"*
5	Saya Ande	*"I'm Ande"*

Dialogue Between Bob and Ande Introducing Themselves:

Setting: Bob and Ande meet for the first time. In this dialogue, Bob and *Ande* introduce themselves and exchange a few basic details about their backgrounds. It's a polite and friendly way to start a conversation when meeting someone in Indonesia, Jakarta.

Bob: (Halo, saya Bob. Senang bertemu denganmu..) – *"Hello, I'm Bob. Nice to meet you."*

Ande: (Halo, Bob. Saya Andy. Senang bertemu denganmu juga..) – *"Hello, Bob. I'm Andy. Nice to meet you too."*

Simple Phrase:

	Indonesian	English
1	Terima kasih kembali	*"You're welcome"*
2	Dari mana asalmu?	*"Where are you from?"*

	Saya dari Indonesia	*"I'm from Indonesia."*
3	Saya datang dari	*"I came from."*
4	Oh, Begitu	*"I see"*
5	Indonesia	*"Indonesia*
6	Sangat indah bukan begitu	*is wonderful, isn't it?"*

Bob: (Sama-sama, Ande) – *"You're welcome, Ande."*

(Asalmu dari mana?) – *"Where are you from?"*

Ande: (Saya berasal dari Surabaya) – *"I'm from Surabaya."*

Bob: (oh, Begitu) – *"I see,"*

(Indonesia itu luar biasa, bukan begitu?.) – *"Indonesia is wonderful, isn't it?"*

Take note: The phrase "*You're welcome*" has two version (Terima kasih Kembali/(Sama-sama), both has the same meaning to express "*You're welcome*".

Simple Phrase:

	Indonesian	English
1	Iya	*"Yes"*
2	Sangat	*"Very"*
3	Kota menarik	*"Interesting city."*
4	Kamu dari mana?	*"Where are you from?"*
5	Saya datang dari	*"I came from"*
6	Saya dari Amerika Serikat	*"I'm from the United States."*
7	Itu menarik	*"That's interesting"*

Ande: (Ya, ini adalah kota yang sangat menarik.) – *"Yes, it's a very interesting city."*

(Kamu berasal dari mana, Bob?) – *"Where are you from, Bob?"*

Bob: (Saya berasal dari Amerika Serikat.) – *"I'm from the United States."*

Bob: (Selamat datang.) – *"Welcome"*

Recall: The Indonesian phrase and understand the English translation

1 Saya Bob

I'm Bob

2 Senang bertemu dengan mu

Nice to meet you.

3 Saya Ande

I'm Ande

4 Terima kasih

Thank you very much

5 Sama-sama

You're welcome

6 Kamu dari mana?

Where are you from?

7 Saya datang dari

I came from

8 Saya dari Indonesia
I'm from Indonesia

9 Oh, Begitu
I see

10 Indonesia sangat menarik
Indonesia is wonderful

11 Ini menarik
It's interesting

12 Kamu dari mana?
Where are you from?

13 Saya dari Amerika Serikat
I'm from the United States.

Lesson 6: How are you?

Here are some basic phrases that you can master and use in any situation, especially when meeting people.

Here is a simple phrase to use if you want to say, "*How are you*?"

1. (Apa kabar?).- "How are you?"

Common Replies:

1. (Iya, Saya sehat.) - "*Yes, I'm well.*"
2. (Saya tidak sehat.) - "*No, I'm not well.*"
3. (Baik saja) – *"I'm good"*

Essential Phrase:

	Indonesian	English
1	Apa kabar?	*"How are you?"*
2	Iya, Saya sehat	*"Yes, I'm well"*
3	Terima kasih	*"Thank you"*
4	Tidak	*"No"*

5	Saya tidak sehat	*"I'm not well"*
6	Kamu gimana?	*"How about you?"*
7	Terima kasih kepadamu	*"Thanks to you"*

These are some typical ways to ask about someone's well-being and respond in Indonesian

Dialogue Between Bob and Ande About Their Health:

Setting: Bob and Ande meet again and ask about each other's health.

Bob: (Halo, Andy. Apa kabar?) – "*Hello, Andy. How are you?*"

Andy: (Halo, Bob. Ya, saya baik-baik saja, terima kasih..) – "*Hello, Bob. Yes, I'm well, thank you.*"

(Kamu gimana?) – "*How about you?*"

Bob: (Terima kasih kepadamu.) – "*Thanks to you,*"

(Saya sehat) – "*I'm well.*"

Recall: The Indonesian phrase and understand the English translation

1 Apa khabar?

How are you?

2 Iya baik

Yes, I'm well.

3 Iya, Saya seha
Yes, I'm well.

4 Tidak, Saya tidak sehat
No, I'm not well.

5 Kamu gimana?
How about you?

6 Terima kasih kepadamu, Saya sehat。
Thanks to you, I'm well.

Lesson 7: What is this?

The phrase "What is this?" in Indonesian can be expressed as:

Essential Phrase

1. (Apa ini?)- "What is this?"

You can use this phrase when you want to ask about the identity or name of an object or thing. So, if you don't know a phrase or item at a shop, just say this phrase, the more you ask the locals, you get more answers and expand your vocabulary.

Reply by saying:

Itu [item]

That is [item]

Simple Phrase:

	Indonesian	**English**
1	Apa ini?	*"What is this?"*

2	Hai	*"Hey"*
3	Ini buku	*"This is a book."*
4	Ini buku tulis	*"This is a writing book."*
5	Ini pena	*"This is a pen."*
6	Ini majallah	*"This is a magazine"*
7	muffin blueberry	*"a blueberry muffin"*
8	Bagaimana dengan ini?	*"What about this?"*
9	croissant cokelat	*"a chocolate croissant"*
10	Saya hanya ingin kopi.	*"I just want a coffee"*
11	Ada lagi?	*"Anything else?"*
12	Tidak, itu saja.	*"No, that's all"*

Dialogue Between Bob and vendor Asking, "What is This?"

Setting: Bob is at stationery store, exploring various items. He approaches the vendor.

Bob: (Permisi, ini apa?) – "*Excuse me, what is this?*"

Vendor: (Ini buku) – *"This is a book."*

(Ini buku tulis) – *"This is a writing book."*

(Ini pena) – *"This is a pen."*

(Ini majallah) – *"This is a magazine."*

Bob: (Apa ini?) – " *What is this?*"

Vendor: (Hah? Itu peta) – *"Huh? That's a map."*

Bob: (Oh, begitu.) – *"Oh, I see."*

Bob: (Saya faham, Saya ambil satu. tolong) – "*I understand, I'll take one, please.*"

Settings: Ande is at the Café, he wants to order something

Barista: (Bisa saya bantu?) – *"Can I help you?"*

Ande: (Iya, Apa ini?) – *"Yes, what is this?"*

Barista: (Itu muffin blueberry) – *"That's a blueberry muffin."*

Ande: (Oh, dan bagaimana dengan ini?) – *"Oh, and what about this?"*

Barista: (Itu croissant cokelat) – *"That's a chocolate croissant."*

Ande: (Terima kasih) – *"Thank you."*

Saya hanya ingin kopi – *"I just want a coffee, please."*

Barista: (Terima kasih) – *"You're welcome."*

(Ada lagi?) – *"anything else?"*

Ande: (Tidak, itu saja) – *"No, that's all."*

(Terima kasih) – *"Thank you"*

Recall: The Indonesian phrase and understand the English translation

1 Apa ini?

What is this?

2 Ini buku
This is a book.

3 Ini buku tulis
This is a writing book.

4 Ini pena
This is a pen.

5 Ini majallah
This is a magazine.

6 Ini peta
That's a map.

7 Begitu
I see

8 Saya faham
I understand

9 Saya ambil satu. tolong
I'll take one, please.

Lesson 8: Who are you?

The phrase "Who are you?" in Indonesian can be expressed as:

Essential Phrase:

1. (Siapa kamu?) – "Who are you?"
2. (Siapa dia?) – "Who is he?"
3. (Siapa dia?) – "Who is she?"

This phrase is a straightforward way to ask someone about their identity or to inquire who they are.

The reply is easy;

For no 1; (Saya Bob) – "**I** am Bob"
For no 2, (Dia Ande) – "**He** is Ande"
For no 3, (Dia Sara) – "**She** is Sara"

If you want to describe the person you can add

1) (pelajar) – *"Student"*
2) (Guru) – *"Teacher"*

Let us observe some sentences;

1) (Dia pelajar) – *"He is a student"*
2) (Dia Guru) – *"She is a teacher"*

Simple Phrase:

	Indonesian	English
1	Siapa kamu?	"Who are you?"
2	Saya Bob	*"I'm Bob"*
3	Senang menemu anda	*"Nice to meet you"*
4	Apa yang kamu lakukan?	*"What do you do?"*
5	Saya pelajar	*"I'm a student"*
6	Belajar	*"Studying"*
7	Universitas	*"University"*
8	Saya belajar di Universitas	*"I'm studying Japanese at university"*
9	Itu luar biasa	*"That's wonderful."*

Dialogue Between Teacher Asking Bob, "Tell me about yourself":

Setting: Bob is a new student in a class, and the teacher is getting to know him. In this dialogue, the teacher asks Bob who he is and what he does, and Bob provides information about himself as a student studying Indonesian.

Teacher: (Siapa kamu?) – "*Hello, who are you?*"

Bob: (Halo, Saya Bob.) –"*Hello, I'm Bob.*"

Teacher: (Senang menemu anda) – "*Nice to meet you, Bob.*"

(Terangkan tentang dirimu?) – *"Tell me about yourself?"*

Bob: (Saya pelajar.) – "*I'm a student.*"

(Saya sedang belajar Indonesia di universitas.) – *"I'm studying Indonesian at the university."*

Teacher: (Itu luar biasa) – "*That's wonderful.*"

Recall: The Indonesian phrase and understand the English translation

1 Siapa kamu?

"*Who are you?*"

2 Senang menemu anda
" *Nice to meet you.*"

3 Apa yang kamu lakukan?
"*What do you do?*"

4 Saya pelajar
"*I'm a student.*"

5 Saya sedang belajar Indonesia di universitas。

"I'm a student. I'm studying Indonesian at the university."

6 Itu luar biasa
"That's wonderful."

Lesson 9: Who is this?

The phrase "Who is this?" in Indonesian can be expressed as:

Essential Phrase:

1. (Siapa ini?) Who is this?

This phrase is used to ask for the identity of a person or inquire about someone you are not familiar with.

Simple Phrase:

	Indonesian	English
1	Siapa ini?	*"Who is this?"*
2	Guru	*"Teacher"*
3	Ini teman saya	*"This is my friend"*
4	Senang menemu anda	*"Nice to meet you"*
5	Ini	*"This is"*
6	Petugas	*"The clerk"*

Dialogue Between Teacher, Bob, and Ande:

Setting: Bob is introducing Ande *to his teacher.* In this dialogue, Bob introduces Ande, and they exchange greetings. The teacher initially asks, "Who is this?" to get to know Ande's identity.

Teacher: (Halo, Bob. Ini siapa?) – "*Hello, Bob. Who is this?*"

Bob: (Halo, Bu Guru. Ini teman saya, Ande..) – "*Hello, teacher. This is my friend, Ande.*"

Teacher: (Senang bertemu denganmu, Ande.) – "*Nice to meet you, Ande.*"

Ande: (Senang bertemu dengan Anda, Pak guru..) – *"Nice to meet you, teacher (male teacher)"*

Bob: (Pak Guru. Siapakah ini?") – *"Teacher. Who is this?"*

Teacher: (Ini petugasnya.) – "*This is the clerk.*"

Teacher: (Ini manajernya.) – "*This is the manager.*"

Ande: (Selamat berkenalan) – *"Nice to know you"*

Siapa itu? – "Who is that?"

Teacher: Itu direktor – "That is the director"

Recall: The Indonesian phrase and understand the English translation

1 Siapakah ini?

" *Who is this?*"

2 Ini teman Saya、
"This is my friend"

3 Senang bertemu denganmu
"*Nice to meet you,"*

4 Siapakah ini?
"Who is this?"

6 Ini Petugas
"*This is the clerk.*"

6 Ini Manajer
"*This is the manager.*"

Lesson 10: Where do you live?

The phrase "Where do you live?" in Indonesian is:

Essential Phrase:

1. (Kamu tinggal di mana?) *Where do you live?*

If you intend to reply. "*I live in*" in Indonesia, you can use the following phrase:

2. (Saya tinggal [location])

Just replace the [location] with the name of the place where you live. For example:

- (Saya tinggal di Indonesia) – "*I live in Indonesia.*"
- (Saya tinggal di Amerika Serikat..) – "*I live in the United States.*"

Simple Phrase:

Indonesian	English

1	Kamu tinggal di mana?	*"Where do you live?"*
2	Saya tinggal di Indonesia	*"I live in Indonesia."*
3	Apakah itu di Jakarta?	*"Is it at Jakarta?"*
4	Bagaimana denganmu?	*"How about You?"*
5	Saya tinggal di Amerika Serikat	*"I live in the United States."*

Dialogue Between Bob and Ande About Where He Lives:

Setting: Bob wants to ask where Ande lives. In this dialogue, Bob asks Ande *where he lives, and* Ande *responds that he lives in Jakarta.*

Bob: (Kamu tinggal di mana?) – "*Where do you live?*"

Ande: (Saya tinggal di Indonesia) – "*I live in Indonesia.*"

Bob: (Oh, jadi itu di Jakarta?) – "*Oh, is it at Jakarta?*

Ande: (Surabaya.) – "*Surabaya*"

Bob: Itu menarik. – "*That is Interesting*"

Bob: Kenapa kamu tinggal di sana? – "*Why do you live there?*"

Ande: Letaknya dekat laut – "*It is near the sea*"

Tempatnya bagus – "*It is a nice place*"

(Bagaimana dengan kamu?.) – "*How about You?*"

Bob: (Saya tinggal di Amerika Serikat – "*I live in the United States.*"

Recall: The Indonesian phrase and understand the English translation

1 Kamu tinggal di mana?
"Where do you live?"

2 Saya tinggal di Indonesia.
"I live in Indonesia."

3 Apakah itu di Jakarta?
"Is it at Jakarta?"

4 Bagaimana denganmu?
"How about You?"

Lesson 11: I speak little Indonesian.

Essential Phrase:

The phrase "I speak little Indonesian" is:

1. (Saya hanya sedikit berbicara bahasa Indonesia) – “I speak little Indonesian”

This phrase can be used when you want to inform someone that you can communicate in basic or simple Indonesian.

Simple Phrase:

	Indonesian	English
1	Saya berbicara bahasa Indonesia sederhana.	*“I Speak simple Indonesian”*
2	Itu luar biasa	*“That's wonderful.”*
3	Bahasa inggris	*“English"*
4	Saya belajar	*“I studied”*

5	Apakah Anda bisa berbahasa Inggris?	*"Can you speak English?"*
6	Ya, saya bisa berbicara sedikit.	*"Yes, I can speak a little."*
7	Itu bagus sekali	*"That's great."*
8	Di mana kamu belajar bahasa Inggris?	*"Where did you learn English?"*
9	Saya belajar bahasa Inggris di universitas	*"I learned English at the university."*

Take note: Neve feel alienated in Indonesia, mixing with the locals by sitting at a food stall (warung) and talking small talk will definitely improve your foreign language acquisition.

Dialogue between Bob and Ande:

Setting: In this dialogue, Bob informs Ande *that he can speak simple Indonesian.*

Bob: (Halo, Ande. Saya berbicara bahasa Indonesia sederhana..) – *"Hello, Ande. I speak simple Indonesian."*

Ande: (Itu luar biasa, Bob.) – *"That's wonderful, Bob."*

Setting: Bob asks Ande if he can speak English and where he learned to speak it.

Bob: (Ande. Bisakah kamu berbicara bahasa Inggris? – *"Ande. Can you speak English?"*

Ande: (Ya, saya bisa berbicara sedikit.) – *"Yes, I can speak a little."*

Bob: (Bagus sekali. Di mana kamu belajar bahasa Inggris?) – *"That's great. Where did you learn English?"*

Ande: (Saya belajar bahasa Inggris di universitas.) – *"I learned English at the university."*

Bob: {Itu bagus sekali) – *"That's great!"*

Ande: **(**Apakah kamu mau berlatih denganku?) – *"Would you like to practice with me?"*

Bob: (Tentu saja, saya sangat ingin. Terima kasih, *Ande*.) – *"Of course, I would love to. Thank you, Ande."*

Recall: The Indonesian phrase and understand the English translation

1 I speak simple Indonesian
"I Speak simple Indonesian"

2 Itu luar biasa
"That's wonderful."

1 bahasa Inggris
"English"

3 Saya Belajar
"I studied/I learned"

4 Bisakah kamu berbicara bahasa Inggris?-
"Can you speak English?"

5 Ya, saya bisa berbicara sedikit
"Yes, I can speak a little."

6 Bagus sekali
"That's great."

7 Di mana kamu belajar bahasa Inggris?
"Where did you learn English?"

8 Saya belajar bahasa Inggris di universitas
"I learned English at the university."

Lesson 12: Rent an apartment.

Students usually rent cheap rooms sharing with friends, we call this (kos-kosan)

Essential Phrase:

The phrase "I want to rent an apartment" is:

1. (Saya **ingin** menyewa apartemen) – "I **want** to rent an apartment"
2. (Saya **mahu** sewa kos-kosan) – "I **want** to rent a boarding house"

Take note: When renting an apartment, you need to pay upfront for a year of rental fees. Whereas student boarding house which cater for students pay on a monthly basis which is much cheaper than an apartment, but the furniture or the walls of the boarding house may look old.

Simple Phrase

Indonesian	**English**

1	Saya ingin menyewa apartemen	*"I want to rent an apartment."*
2	Bisakah kamu membantuku?	*"Can you help me?"*
3	Iya, Bisa	*Yes, I can*
4	Saya Mengerti	*"I Understood"*
5	Mari kita cari apartemen murah.	*"let's look for a cheap apartment."*

Dialogue Between Bob and Ande:

Setting: Bob expresses his desire to rent a cheap apartment.

Bob: (Halo, And. Saya ingin menyewa apartemen.) – "*Hello, Ande. I want to rent an apartment.*"

Bob: (Bisakah kamu membantuku?) – *"Can you help me?"*

Ande: (Saya Mengerti, Mari kita cari apartemen murah.) - *"I Understood, let's look for a cheap apartment."*

Ande: (Apartemen di kawasan perkotaan) - *" Apartment at the city area."*

Ande: (Mahal) – *"Expensive."*

Ande: (Namun daerah pedesaan) – *" But the rural area."*

Ande: (lebih murah) – *" is cheaper."*

Bob: (Saya lebih menyukai kota.) – *"I prefer the city"*

Ande: (Kenapa) – *" why?"*

Bob: (karena fasilitas.) – *"because of amenities"*

Ande: (Iya benar) – *" Yes, that is correct"*

How to express "I want"

In Japanese, you can express "I want" by using the phrase "*Saya ingin*". Simply fill in the blank with the thing you want. For example:

- (Saya ingin makan) - "I want food."
- (Saya ingin mobil) - "I want a car."
- (Saya ingin buku) - "I want a book."

So, to say, "I want" in Indonesian, you use "Saya ingin". and specify what you desire after it. Please take note: that sometimes the locals use the phrase, “Saya Mahu” instead of “Saya ingin” both phrase has the same meaning.

Recall: The Indonesian phrase and understand the English translation

1 Ingin/mahu

“want”

2 Saya ingin makan

"I want food."

3 Saya ingin mobil
"I want a car."

4 Saya ingin buku
"I want a book."

5 Saya ingin sewa apartmen
"I want to rent an apartment."

6 Bisakah kamu membantuku?
"Can you help me?"

7 Saya Mengerti
"I Understood"

8 Mari kita cari apartemen murah
"let's look for a cheap apartment."

Lesson 13: At the café

Here are some simple nouns related to cafes in Indonesian: The phrase is practical for daily conversation.

1. (Kopi) - Coffee
2. (Teh) - Tea
3. (Kue) - Cake
4. (Roti) - Bread
5. (Jus) - Juice
6. (Sandwich) - Sandwich
7. (Menu) - Menu
8. (Pesanan) - Order
9. (Tagihan) - Bill
10. (Meja) - Table
11. (Meja kasir (di bar)) – (Counter (at the bar)
12. (Serbet) - Napkin
13. (Sendok) - Spoon

Essential Phrase:

You can use this phrase when you want to ask someone about their desires or what they would like. The phrase "What do you want?" is:

1. (Kamu mau apa?) – *"What do you want?"*

Reply by saying; (Saya mahu [insert object]) – *"I want* [insert object]*"*

If you don't know the name of the item, just point at the item that you need to order. Isn't that easy. Then you can ask (Apa ini) – *"What is this?"*

The lady may say,

(Bakso) – *"meat ball noodle"*

(Bakwan) – *"fried flour mixed with carrot, cabbage"*

(Ayam penyet) – *"Crispy fried chicken with chili"*

(Ulam) – *"fresh mixed vegies"*

Simple Phrase:

Indonesian	**English**

1	Selamat datang	*"Welcome"*
2	Silakan	*"Please"*
3	Kopi panas	*"Hot coffee"*
4	Roti dengan Mentega	*"Bread with Butter"*
5	Tentu	*"Certainly"*
6	Mohon tunggu sebentar	*"Please wait a moment."*

Dialogue Between Bob and the Waitress at the Cafe:

Setting: Bob is in a cafe and expresses his desire for coffee and bread.

Waitress: (Selamat datang.) – "*Welcome.*"

Bob: (Saya pesan kopi panas, ya.) – "*I'd have hot coffee, please.*"

Bob: (Roti dengan mentega, tolong.) – *"Bread with butter, please."*

Waitress: (Tentu. Mohon tunggu sebentar.) – "*Certainly. Please wait a moment.*"

(Ini kopinya) – *"Here is the coffee"*

Waitress: (Apa lagi.) – "*What else.*"

Bob: (Telor setengah matang.) – *"Half-boiled eggs"*

In Indonesia, half boiled eggs usually eaten with soya ketchup and white pepper.

Recall: The Indonesian phrase and understand the English translation

1 Kamu mau apa?

"What do you want?"

2 Selamat datang

"Welcome."

3 Saya pesan kopi panas, ya
"I'd have hot coffee, please."

4 Roti dengan mentega, tolong
"Bread with butter, please."

5 Tentu
"Certainly."

6 Mohon tunggu sebentar
"Please wait a moment."

Lesson 14: Where is the grocery store?

Here are some common nouns related to grocery store items.

1. (Sayuran) - Vegetables
2. (Buah-buahan) - Fruits
3. (Beras) – Rice (sold in bags)
4. (Nasi) – Rice (cooked and ready to eat)
5. (Roti) - Bread
6. (Susu) - Milk
7. (Telur) - Eggs
8. (Daging) - Meat
9. (Ikan) - Fish
10. (Makanan ringan) - Snacks
11. (Jus) - Juice
12. (Mie) - Noodles
13. (Keju) - Cheese
14. (Rempah-rempah) - Spices
15. (Pasta) - Pasta

These nouns represent a variety of food items and products you might typically find when shopping at a grocery store.

Essential Phrase:

	Indonesian	English
1	Supermarket	*"Supermarket"*
2	toko kelontong	*"Grocery store"*
3	Pasar	*"Wet market"*
4	Minimarket	*"Mini mart"*
5	Warung makan	*"Food stalls"*
6	wartek	*"Café"*

The phrase "Where is it?" in Indonesian is:

1. (Di mana letaknya?) – "*Where is it?*"
2. (Di mana letak supermarketnya?) –"*Where is the supermarket?*"
3. (Dimana pasar?) – "*Where is the market?*"
4. (Di mana letak toko kelontong?) – "*Where is the grocery store?*"

You can use this phrase to ask for the location of a market, you will find out that most market in Indonesia sells all types of dry food, seeds, fish and more

Take note:

The word "Grocery store" sometimes refers to (toko kelontong) and (toko pangan,)

Dialogue Between Bob and the Ande at Bob's rented apartment:

Setting: Bob needs to buy some basic necessities to store food.

Bob: (Permisi, di mana toko pangan?) – *"Excuse me, where is the grocery store?"*

Ande: (Terletak di jalan utama) – *"It is on the main road"*

Ande (Anda mau beli apa?) – *"What are you buying?"*

Bob: (Saya butuh sembako). – *"I need necessities"*

Ande (Dan apa saja itu) – *"And what's that?"*

Bob: (Beras, mie, tepung, telur, sayuran.) – *"Rice, Noodles, Flour, eggs, vegetables"*

Recall: The Indonesian phrase and understand the English translation

1 Toko kelontong

"Grocery store"

2 Pasar
"market"

3 Minimarket
"Mini mart"

4 Warung makan
"Food stalls"

5 Di mana letaknya?
"*Where is it?*"

6 Di mana letak toko kelontong?
"*Where is the grocery store?*"

7 Di mana letak pasar?
"*Where is the market?*"

Lesson 15: Where is the train station?

It is normal to counter a situation when you need to ask around and meet new people, don't be afraid to ask people on the streets for directions.

Essential Phrase:

The phrase "Where is the train station?" in Indonesian is:

1. (Di mana letak stasiun kereta api?)

Here are some common transportation nouns in Indonesian:

1. (Mobil) - Car
2. (Sepeda) - Bicycle
3. (Bis) - Bus
4. (Kereta api) - Train
5. (terowongan) - Subway
6. (Taksi) - Taxi
7. (Pesawat) - Airplane
8. (Sepeda motor) - Bike/Motorbike
9. (stasiun) - Station
10. (Bandara) - Airport
11. (halte bis) - Bus stop
12. (Tiket) - Ticket

Simple Phrase:

	Indonesian	English
1	(Mobil)	*"Car"*
2	Di mana mobilnya?	*"Where is the car?"*
3	(sepeda)	*"Bicycle"*
4	Di mana sepedanya?	*"Where is the bicycle?"*
5	(Bis)	*"Bus"*
6	Di mana bisnya?	*"Where is the bus?"*
7	Di mana kereta apinya ?	*"Where is the train?"*
8	Kereta api ada di sana.	*"The train is over there."*

Dialogue between Bob and train master about the train.

Settings: Bob is confused and ask for help.

Bob: (Permisi, di mana keretanya?) – "*Excuse me, where is the train?*"

Train Master: (Kereta api ada di sana.) – "*The train is over there.*"

Train Master: (Kamu mahu kemana?) – "*Where are you going?*"

Bob: (Saya mahu ke Surabaya) – "*I want to go to Surabaya.*"

Train Master: (Beli tiket di loket.) – "*Buy a ticket at the counter*"

Train Master: (Turun di stasiun Jember) – "*Get off at Jember station.*"

Bob: (Terima kasih banyak) – "*Thank you very much.*"

Train Master: (Sama-sama) – "*You are welcome.*"

Settings: Bob return home and ask Ande some questions related to travel to Surabaya.

Bob: (Apakah bisa ke Surabaya dengan menaiki pesawat) – *"Is it possible to go to Surabaya by plane?"*

Ande: (Iya tentu) – *"Yes, of course"*

(Dari Jakarta, Bandara Soekarno Hatta dan turun di Bandara Juanda) – *"from Jakarta, Soekarno Hatta Airport and get off at Juanda Airport"*

Bob: (Bisa kamu ikut denganku ke Surabaya?) – *"Can you go with me to Surabaya?"*

Ande: (Iya tentu) – *"Yes, of course"*

Note: The word (Bisa) means "can"

Recall: The Indonesian phrase and understand the English translation

1 Di mana letak stasiun kereta api?)
"*Where is the train station?*"

2 Mobil
"Car"

3 Sepeda
"Bicycle"

4 Bis
"Bus"

5 Kereta Api
"Train"

6 Terowong
"Subway"

7 Taksi
"Taxi"

8 Pesawat
"Airplane"

9 stasiun
"Station"

10 Bandara
"Airport"

11 halte bis
"Bus stop"

12 Di mana mobil?
"Where is the car?"

13 Di mana sepeda?
"Where is the bicycle?"

14 Di mana bisn?
"Where is the bus?"

15 Di mana kereta api?
"Where is the train?"

16 Kereta api ada di sana
"The train is over there"

Phrase Builder-RECALL WHATEVER YOU HAVE LEARNT

Lesson 1: Common Greetings	
Halo	*"Hello "*
Selamat pagi	*"Good morning."*
Selamat siang	*"Good afternoon"*
Selamat sore	*"Good evening"*
Selamat malam	*"Good night"*
sampai berjumpa lagi	*"See you soon"*
Selamat tinggal	*"Goodbye"*
Iya	*"Yes"*
Tidak/Ngak	*"No"*
Maaf	*"I'm sorry"*
Gimana hari mu?	*"How's your day?"*
Hari ini bagus	*"My day is good"*
Terima kasih sebab bertanya	*"Thank you for asking"*
Baik	*"Well,"*
Saya harus pergi sekarang	*"I have to go now"*
Terima kasih atas ngombrolan	*"Thank you for the conversation"*
Sama-sama	*"You're welcome!"*
Jumpa lagi	*"See you later."*

Lesson 2: Expressing Gratitude

Ini dia	*"Here is "*
Kopi anda	*"Your coffee."*
Teh anda	*"Your Tea."*
Terima kasih	*"Thank you"*
Terima kasih kembali	*"You're welcome"*
Gula	*"Sugar"*
Krimer	*"Creamer"*
Bisa Saya dbantu Anda?"	*"Can I help you?"*
secangkir kopi	*"a coffee"*
omelet	*"an omelette"*
Saya ingin kopi dan omelet.	*"I would like a coffee and an omelette"*
Tolong	*"please"*
Sebentar	*"a moment"*

Lesson 3: Apologizing

Saya minta maaf	*"I'm sorry_"*
Aku terlambat	*"I'm late."*

Saya ingin meminta bantuan.	*"I have a favour to ask"*
Tidak, tidak apa-apa.	*"No, it's okay"*
Aku benar-benar minta maaf	*"I'm really sorry"*
Bolehkah saya duduk disini?	*"May I sit here?"*
sama sekali tidak mengapa	*"Absolutely no problem"*
Tolong	*"Please"*
Duduklah bersamaku	*"Sit with me."*
Terima kasih banyak	*"Thank you very much"*
Tidak masalah	*"No worries"*

Lesson 4: Introduce someone	
Ini	*"This is"*
Buku Bob	*"Bob's book"*
Teman Mary	*"Mary's friend"*
Mobil Tom	*"Tom's car"*
Abang saya	*"My brother"*

Encantado de conocer	*"Nice to meet you."*
Kemeja John	*"John's shirt"*
Sepeda Thomas	*"Thomas' motorbike"*
Kacamata Sheila	*"Sheila's glasses"*
Ponsel John	*"John's mobile phone"*
Kamera Daniel	*"Daniel's camera"*

Lesson 5: What's your name?	
Saya	*"I am"*
[Nama anda]	*[Your Name].*
Dan kamu?	*"And you?"*
Saya John	*"I am John."*
Saya Bob	*"I'm Bob"*
Senang temu anda	*"Nice to meet you."*
Halo, Bob	*"Hello, Bob."*
Terima kasih kembali	*"You're welcome"*
Saya Ande	*"I'm Ande"*
Dari mana asalmu?	*Where are you from?*

Saya dari Indonesia	*I'm from Indonesia.*
Saya datang dari	*"I came from."*
Oh, Begitu	*I see*
Indonesia	*Indonesia*
Sangat indah bukan begitu	*is wonderful, isn't it?*
Iya	*"Yes"*
Sangat	*"Very"*
Kota menarik	*"Interesting city."*
Kamu dari mana?	*"Where are you from?"*
Saya datang dari	*"I came from"*
Saya dari Amerika Serikat	*"I'm from the United States."*
Itu menarik	*"That's interesting"*

Lesson 6: How are you?	
Apa kabar?	*"How are you?"*
Iya, Saya sehat	*"Yes, I'm well"*
Terima kasih	*"Thank you"*
Tidak	*"No"*
Saya tidak sehat	*"I'm not well"*
Kamu gimana?	*"How about you?"*
Terima kasih kepadamu	*"Thanks to you"*

Lesson 7: What’s is this?	
Apa ini?	*"What is this?"*
Hai	*"Hey"*
Ini buku	*"This is a book."*
Ini buku tulis	*"This is a writing book."*
Ini pena	*"This is a pen."*
Ini majallah	*"This is a magazine"*
muffin blueberry	*"a blueberry muffin"*
Bagaimana dengan ini?	*"What about this?"*
croissant cokelat	*"a chocolate croissant"*
Saya hanya ingin kopi.	*"I just want a coffee"*
Ada lagi?	*"Anything else?"*
Tidak, itu saja.	*"No, that's all"*

Lesson 8: Who are you?	

Siapa kamu?	"Who are you?"
Saya Bob	*"I'm Bob"*
Senang menemu anda	*"Nice to meet you"*
Apa yang kamu lakukan?	*"What do you do?"*
Saya pelajar	*"I'm a student"*
Belajar	*"Studying"*
Universitas	*"University"*
Saya belajar di Universitas	*"I'm studying Japanese at university"*
Itu luar biasa	*"That's wonderful."*

Lesson 9: Who is this?

Siapa ini?	*"Who is this?"*
Guru	*"Teacher"*
Ini teman saya	*"This is my friend"*
Senang menemu anda	*"Nice to meet you"*
Ini	*"This is"*
Petugas	*"The clerk"*
Manējā desu	*"The manager"*

insinyur perangkat lunak	"a software engineer"
Saya bekerja	"I work"
Saya bekerja sebagai insinyur perangkat lunak.	"I work as a software engineer"
Itu menarik	*"That's interesting"*
Apa spesialisasi Anda?	*"What's your specialization?"*
Saya berspesialisasi	*"I specialize"*
perkembangan	*"development"*
dalam pengembangan aplikasi seluler	*"in mobile app development"*
Siapa nama kamu?	*"What is your name?"*
apa warna kesukaanmu	*"What is your favorite color?"*
apa makanan kesukaanmu	*"What is your favorite food?"*
Apa nombor ponsel mu?	*"What is your phone number?"*
Apa film favoritmu?	*"What is your favorite movie?"*
Siapa	*"Who"*
Siapa dia?	*"Who is he?"*

Siapa orang itu?	*"Who is that man?"*
Siapa kamu?	*"Who are you?"*
Siapa teman karib kamu	*"Who is your best friend?"*
Kapan	*"When"*
Kapan ulang tahunmu?	*"When is your birthday?"*
Kapan kita bisa bertemu?	*"When can we meet?"*
Kapan kita akan pergi ke taman?	*"When are we going to the park?"*
Kapan filmnya mulai?	*"When does the movie start?"*

Lesson 10: Where do you live?	
Kamu tinggal di mana?	*"Where do you live?"*
Saya tinggal di Indonesia	*"I live in Indonesia."*
Apakah itu di Jakarta?	*"Is it at Jakarta?"*

Bagaimana denganmu?	*"How about You?"*
Saya tinggal di Amerika Serikat	*"I live in the United States."*
menarik	*"Interesting."*
kenapa	*"Why?"*
laut	*"Sea"*
dekat	*"Near"*
Tempat bagus	*"nice place"*

Lesson 11: I Speak little Indonesian	
Saya berbicara bahasa Indonesia sederhana.	*"I Speak simple Indonesian"*
Itu luar biasa	*"That's wonderful."*
Bahasa inggris	*"English"*
Saya belajar	*"I studied"*
Apakah Anda bisa berbahasa Inggris?	*"Can you speak English?"*
Ya, saya bisa berbicara sedikit.	*"Yes, I can speak a little."*
Itu bagus sekali	*"That's great."*

Di mana kamu belajar bahasa Inggris?	*"Where did you learn English?"*
Saya belajar bahasa Inggris di universitas	*"I learned English at the university."*
Itu menarik	*"That's interesting!"*
Saya bisa berbicara	*"I can speak"*
sedikit	*"a little"*
Itu bagus sekali	*"That's great."*
berlatih	*"Practice"*
denganku	*"With me"*
Apakah kamu mau berlatih denganku?	*"Would you like to practice with me?"*
Tentu saja	*"Of course,"*
saya sangat ingin	*"I would love to"*

Lesson 12: I want to rent	
Saya ingin menyewa apartemen	*"I want to rent an apartment."*

Bisakah kamu membantuku?	*"Can you help me?"*
Iya, Bisa	*Yes, I can*
Saya Mengerti	*"I Understood"*
Mari kita cari apartemen murah.	*"let's look for a cheap apartment."*
kota	*city*
kawasan	*"area"*
Mahal	*"Expensive."*
Namun	*But*
daerah pedesaan	*the rural area."*
lebih murah	*'is cheaper"*
Saya lebih menyukai kota	*"I prefer the city"*
Kenapa	*" Why?"*
karena fasilitas	*"because of amenities"*
Iya benar	*"Yes, that is correct"*

Lesson 13: At the café	
Kopi	*"Coffee."*
Cangkir	*"Cup"*
Susu	*"Milk"*

Gula	*“Sugar”*
Sendok	*"Spoon”*
Agua	*"Water”*
Teh	*“Tea”*
kueh	*“Cake”*
Biskut	*"Cookie"*
Minuman ringan	*"Soft drink."*
Serbet	*“Napkin"*
Roti	*"Bread"*
mentega	*"Butter"*
Jus	*"Juice"*
Say mau	*“I want”*
Selamat datang	*“Welcome”*
Silakan	*“Please”*
Kopi panas	*“Hot coffee”*
Roti dengan Mentega	*“Bread with Butter”*
Tentu	*“Certainly”*
Mohon tunggu sebentar	*“Please wait a moment."*
Saya pesan kopi panas, ya	*"I'd have hot coffee, please”*
Roti dengan mentega, tolong	*"Bread with butter, please."*
Tentu. Mohon tunggu sebentar	*"Certainly. Please wait a moment”*
Ini kopinya	*"Here is the coffee”*
Apa lagi	*"What else”*

Telor setengah matang	*"Half-boiled eggs"*
Kue coklat	*"Chocolate cake"*
Berikut pesanan Anda	*"Here is* Your order"
Datang lagi	*"Come again"*

Lesson 14: Where is the grocery store?	
Sayuran	*"Vegetables."*
Buah-buahan	*"Fruits"*
Beras	*"Rice in a pack"*
Roti	*"Bread"*
Susu	*"Milk"*
Telur	*"Eggs"*
Daging	*"Meat"*
Makanan ringan	*"Snacks."*
Mie	*"Noodles."*
Keju	*"Cheese."*
Rempah-rempah	*"Spices."*
Pasta	*"Pasta"*
Supermarket	*"Supermarket"*
toko kelontong	*"Grocery store"*
Pasar	*"Wet market"*
Minimarket	*"Mini mart"*

Warung makan	*"Food stalls"*
wartek	*"Café"*
Di mana letak supermarketnya?	*"Where is the supermarket?"*
Dimana pasar?	*"Where is the market?"*
Di mana letak toko kelontong	*"Where is the grocery store?"*
Permisi, di mana toko pangan?	*"Excuse me, where is the grocery store?"*
Terletak di jalan utama	*"It is on the main road"*
Anda mau beli apa?)	*"What are you buying?"*
Saya butuh sembako.	*"I need necessities"*
Dan apa saja itu?	*"And what's that?"*
Beras, mie, tepung, telur, sayuran	*"Rice, Noodles, Flour, eggs, vegetables"*

Lesson 15: Where is the train station?

Mobil	*"Car "*
Sepeda	*"Bicycle"*
Bis	*"Bus"*
Kereta api	*"Train"*
terowongan	*"Subway"*
Taksi	*"Taxi"*
Pesawat	*"Airplane"*
Sepeda motor	*"Motorbike"*
stasiun	*"Station"*
halte bis	*"Bus stop"*
Tiket	*"Ticket"*
Di mana mobil?	*"Where is the car?"*
Di mana sepeda?	*"Where is the bicycle?"*
Di mana bisn?	*"Where is the bus?"*
Di mana kereta api?	*"Where is the train?"*
Kereta api ada di sana.	*"The train is over there."*
Kamu mahu kemana?	*"Where are you going?"*
Saya mahu ke Surabaya	*"I want to go to Surabaya."*
Beli tiket di loket	*Buy a ticket at the counter"*
Turun di stasiun Jember	*"Get off at Jember station."*

Apakah bisa ke Surabaya dengan menaiki pesawat	*"Is it possible to go to Surabaya by plane?"*
Iya tentu	*"Yes, of course"*
Dari Jakarta, Bandara Soekarno Hatta dan turun di Bandara Juanda	*"from Jakarta, Soekarno Hatta Airport and get off at Juanda Airport"*
Bisakah kamu ikut denganku ke Surabaya?)	*"Can you go with me to Surabaya?"*
Iya tentu	*"Yes, of course"*

Last Words from the Author.

"We have invested hours structuring this book for lower beginner's standard, to help you easily master the Indonesian language. But we add some spices to your learning journey, that is to get more Indonesian resource on our website: LETS-360.com

We hope this small handbook has led you to the discovery of the Indonesian language, keep it up, you are on the way to master Indonesian. Don't forget to look for the next series for level 2.

If you know people who want to learn, why not try our books.

Send this book link to your friends, perhaps they are interested in learning a new foreign language just like you. Cheers!"

From the desk of
Mohd Mursalin Sa’ad
Damascus, Syria

Get more Resource

Study planner

Conversation writing material

And more

At lets-360.com

www.ingramcontent.com/pod-product-compliance
Lightning Source LLC
LaVergne TN
LVHW101616210926
848480LV00009B/659